DEBUT

YVES SAINT LAURENT
1962

Project Manager, English-language edition: Ellen Nidy
Editor, English-language edition: Matthew Giles
Design coordinator, English-language edition: Tina Thompson
Translated from the French by Alexandra Bonfante-Warren

Library of Congress Control Number: 2001098135
ISBN 0-8109-0561-2

Printed and bound in France

10 9 8 7 6 5 4 3 2 1

Harry N. Abrams, Inc.
100 Fifth Avenue
New York, N.Y. 10011
www.abramsbooks.com

Abrams is a subsidiary of

DEBUT

YVES SAINT LAURENT
1962

Photographs by Pierre Boulat

Text by Laurence Benaïm

Captions by Pierre Bergé

Harry N. Abrams, Inc., Publishers

YVES SAINT LAURENT

A Fire Maker

"For more than six weeks, from a corner of the atelier, I witnessed the preparation of Yves Saint Laurent's first collection—a brilliant opportunity for a photographer."

Winter 1961: thirty-seven-year-old *Life* photographer Pierre Boulat shuttled between some two hundred square meters of converted maids' rooms, the rue Spontini showrooms, and the two-room rue La Boétie apartment, tracking the preparations for the stunning debut collection from Yves Saint Laurent's couture house. *Life*'s French correspondent, Boulat had been dragged to Port Saïd, Algiers, and West Point before he landed in the heart of Paris's 8th arrondissement, where Saint Laurent coached a young team of a half-dozen less-than-thirty-year-olds, sponsored by an American financier from Atlanta. Indeed, a first in Paris: an American businessman, J. Mack Robinson (whose name would remain a secret until 1963), invested $700,000 to open the house.

"When I look at Saint Laurent, all I see is Orson Welles. That same profound sincerity, nothing phony," Boulat later said. His more than 250 shots documented an intimate and theatrical adventure experienced amid the anticipation, concentration, and doubts of that first "terrible year" that Victoire, a former Dior model, would later recount. Pierre Bergé hurled himself into the fray, convinced that Marc Bohan, the designer who had replaced Saint Laurent at Dior, posed no great threat. And he knew that "neither Balenciaga nor Chanel could keep a young man of twenty-five from exploding." Bergé had sold his apartment on rue Saint-Louis-en-l'Île and some paintings by Bernard Buffet, whose "miserabilist period," was, as luck would have it, prized by collectors at the time.

In July 1961, Bergé rented an apartment at 66 rue La Béotie to use as an atelier and bought a desk and a few chairs from a flea market. He commissioned the graphic artist Cassandre to design a logo. Saint Laurent drew his first sketches on a wood panel while Bergé hired the staff. Half of the twenty-four seamstresses came from Dior. The idea was to open a small house with a "big name." Boulat recalled: "Everything from the doorknobs to the plumbing had to have the 'YSL' look, Saint Laurent's long fingers caressing metal knobs and exclusive fabrics the same way, or lifting costume-jewelry stones in multicolored ripples." As Boulat saw it, Saint Laurent was very much the "child with nerves of steel" that Mishima would describe two years later, during one of the couturier's trips to Japan. Silently intent on capturing the truth within the mystery, Boulat surprised Saint Laurent by neither betraying nor distracting him.

After the House of Dior thanked him, following his sixth and last— and darkest—collection, Saint Laurent vanished from couture's small universe. The "young man on the flying trapeze" whose first collection, in January 1958, had brought him glory at Dior, discovered privacy, the gift of anonymity. He was drafted into the army, and then discharged for health reasons in November 1960. Six weeks in the quarantine pavilion at Val-de-Grâce, followed by a stay in the Canary Islands with Bergé, with whom he went on to share an apartment in Place Vauban, contributed to Saint Laurent's transformation as he prepared to open his couture house amid the greatest secrecy.

His strength lay in his understanding that the age to which he was responding was no longer one of lines, but of style, of clothing that dressed an attitude, rather than a seasonally dictated silhouette. If Chanel liberated women, Saint Laurent empowered them.

The mystery was fueled by an article in the *Paris Match* of August 5, 1961, entitled "Deux Parisiennes semblent porter du Yves Saint Laurent" [Two Parisiennes appear to be wearing Yves Saint Laurent]. One of the two women was Zizi Jeanmaire, for whom Saint Laurent had just designed 250 costumes, including the famous "feather thing" and the pullover sweater that she wore with dancing shoes on the stage of the Alhambra. The other woman, Dior model Victoire, whose hair was styled in the celebrated pouf created by the hairdresser Alexandre, announced to the elegant ladies: "Yves Saint Laurent is opening his couture house."

Saint Laurent's house was officially inaugurated on December 4, 1961. He rose to the challenge, creating fireworks, invigorated by his desire for beauty—the sole antidote to the "mortal boredom" that Serge Gainsbourg was singing about at the time. "I have an inner strength and a fierce will that push me toward the light," Saint Laurent said. "I'm a fighter and a winner." Never has he doubted either his strength or his talent for sorrow. Fashion had stolen his youth once before—but did he even want to be so young? It was then fashion, once again, that restored his name and glory in letters of gold.

Boulat was the only photographer given entrée into what Monsieur Dior would have called the "daydream office." Here was Saint Laurent standing, sitting, kneeling, crouching to correct a fabric or drape a length of cloth. Evoking the invisible from behind his tortoiseshell Gualdoni glasses, the "bird-man" caresses the shadow of these untouchable women who rise out of his chimerical realm. Black glasses and white cloche. Black chiffon startling against bare skin. Moonstone lace on white cotton. Reality takes shape from within the imagination. Daytime suits, gowns for the theater, and formal evening gowns. Saint Laurent drawing. Counting days from a *Belleville-Reneaux* calendar pinned to the wall. The invisible Boulat witnessed his silent rages: "He was performing a complex pantomime, his apparent calm masking anxiety mixed with the kind of superstitiousness that needs a good-luck charm *du jour*." Boulat, too, concealed an impressive visual

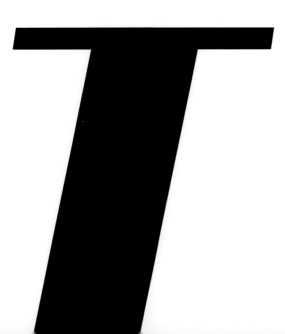

memory beneath the air of perpetual childhood. To this picture-hunter the couturier embodied an artistic spirit that was always at the ready, a craftsman whose course Boulat would follow for thirty years. He immortalized Saint Laurent in an iconic shot that he would repeat in 1982 and 1992: Saint Laurent in a white smock in his atelier, studying his model in the mirror, her increasingly prominent-shouldered silhouette manifesting the curves of the day.

Sometimes the tension is extreme. The scene is set. White-linen-covered walls. Narrow colored ribbons. Fittings take place in tension-filled silence. A pool of black silk on the ground. Madame Esther, hired as first dressmaker, pins the fabric for a skirt on Victoire. All gazes are focused on the mirrors. The collection will be transported by truck during the night of January 29, 1962 to 30 bis rue Spontini, the old Forain atelier, where Yves Saint Laurent discovered a good-luck charm—a ten of clubs—in the basement.

At each instance, Boulat smoothly, gently, parted the moment's veil, explored the shadow of a secret, and entered into this silent choreography—it was the heart of the city, yet far from its din and confusion. "It was incredible that we met," relates Bergé, now president of Yves Saint Laurent Haute Couture, the house whose every moment since 1961 has contributed to an extraordinary and unique story—it established the legend of the two-headed couture eagle, the saga of Saint Laurent and Bergé who would become known as "the two anarchist millionaires," systematically breaking the rules of a trade (of which they are now the last emperors) in the name of the age, of passion, and of a life woven of secrets. "Pierre Boulat was with us practically night and day. We realized we were composing a memoir together. This was the portrait of a man creating his couture house," Bergé relates. Boulat's photographs later appeared in the April 9, 1962, issue of *Life*, under the title "The Comeback of Yves Saint Laurent."

That was forty years ago. In January 2001, Saint Laurent presented his summer 2001 haute couture runway show. Soft, bright colors, powdery yellows, chalky blues, iridescent whipcord grays—the master of the "now" look gave yet another demonstration of his craft. This was the essence of French fashion in its sense of balance and harmony of proportions. The illusion was of colors being glimpsed from beneath a veil, or in fog, for a tailored and precise silhouette. "Haute couture," he said, "is a matter of millimeters, whispered secrets." The artisans seemed to have worked outdoors to achieve effects resembling silken gardens shivering beneath a cloudburst, dresses rippled by breezes, white organdy blouse-whispers like featherweight fabrics ventilating the body even as they delicately emphasized its contours, the shoulders and wrists wreathed in bewitchments. A white organdy coat floated by, festooned with ostrich feathers. The white is both fresh and sensual, neither minimalist nor priestly, lighter than a cloud. To the strains of "Teach Me Tonight" and "Call Me Irresponsible," the voices of Nancy Wilson, Sarah Vaughn, and Dinah Washington serenaded the 105 designs, in a breath evoking other places and moments of happiness. For the finale

Laetitia Casta appeared in a traveling suit, on Saint Laurent's arm, as if leaving on her honeymoon.

From his office at 5 avenue Marceau, Bergé has participated in this long voyage, which recent events—Gucci's takeover of Yves Saint Laurent and the installation of Tom Ford as YSL Rive Gauche's new artistic director—appear to have left untouched. The black-clad "couture" saleswomen pad silently about this house where dresses are displayed below stone cherubs like trophies of velvet and silk. When Saint Laurent climbs the stairs, it is as if a music box starts up. Here, time seems suspended above a solitary being who has dedicated his life to a craft that was not, perhaps, his thing—he who dreamed of the theater and the opera. He is a nomad who has settled down, but who can travel just by looking at a picture, and pursue life in his own haunted castles where life's disorder must always submit to the implacable laws of Beauty, which demands and kills, tolerating nothing but itself. "What endures in Yves," says Bergé, "is his sense of childhood, and his refusal to leave it. His work absorbed him and he took refuge in a coccoon—imaginary or otherwise—which he created totally and which he inhabits full time. Yves is Hölderlin and Rimbaud. A fire maker. This is not to say that he lacks determination: he is endowed with the great will of the weak. Strong people are more pragmatic."

Boulat's strength lay in catching the eternity—and the urgency—of the moment. The sacred part that evades couture's seasons. The birth of a legend. "Those times seem far away," Bergé admits, "because the craft seems far away. Couturiers used to impose fashions—today, they submit to them. If I had it to do again, I wouldn't start over. Who would be crazy enough to open a house of haute couture and dress a dozen rich women?"

Through Boulat's lens, Saint Laurent, seated at a table like an enchanted diamond merchant, plunges his hands, fingers spread star-like, into a river of rhinestones. The first collection was lit by this talisman-heart of real fake rubies, which was pinned onto his favorite design. A heart he has always kept.

LAURENCE BENAÏM

The predator's eye that won't let go of its prey.

OVERLEAF:

Three initials that would travel the globe.

OVERLEAF:

In this, you can see an homage to Chanel.

It all started at that moment.

Which one of us was right?

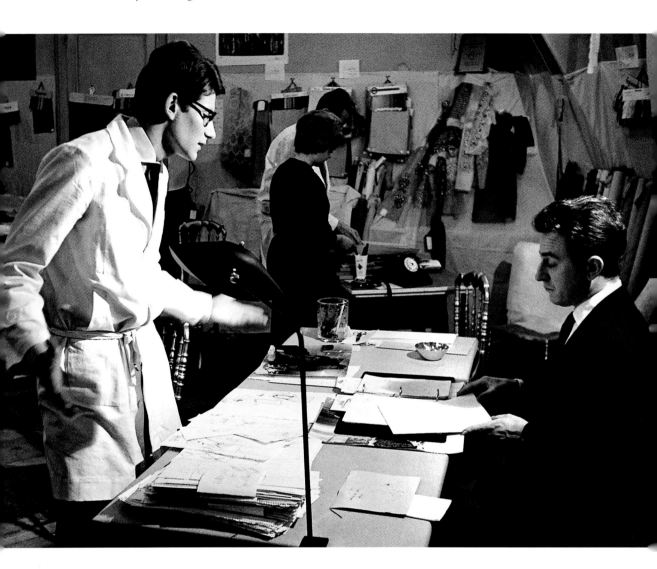

Cassandre hadn't arrived.

… already organized!

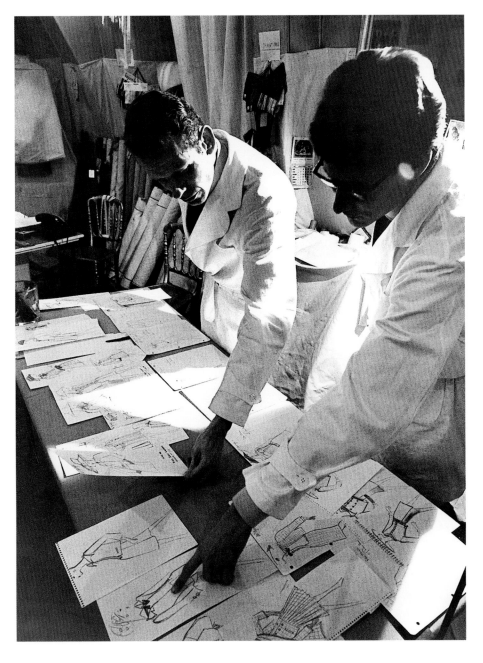

A blanket! It'll become a dress.

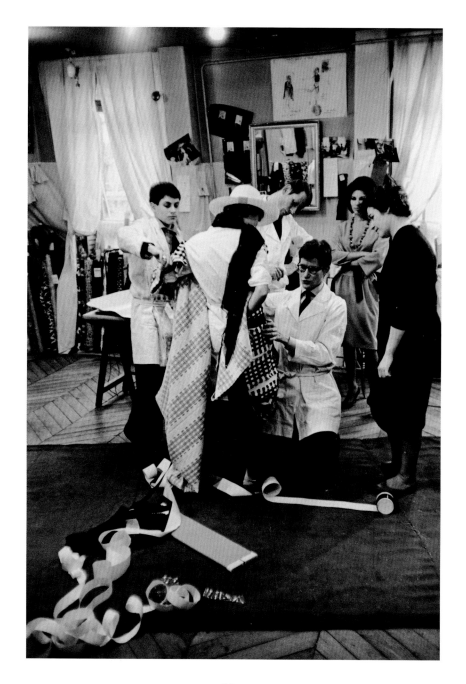

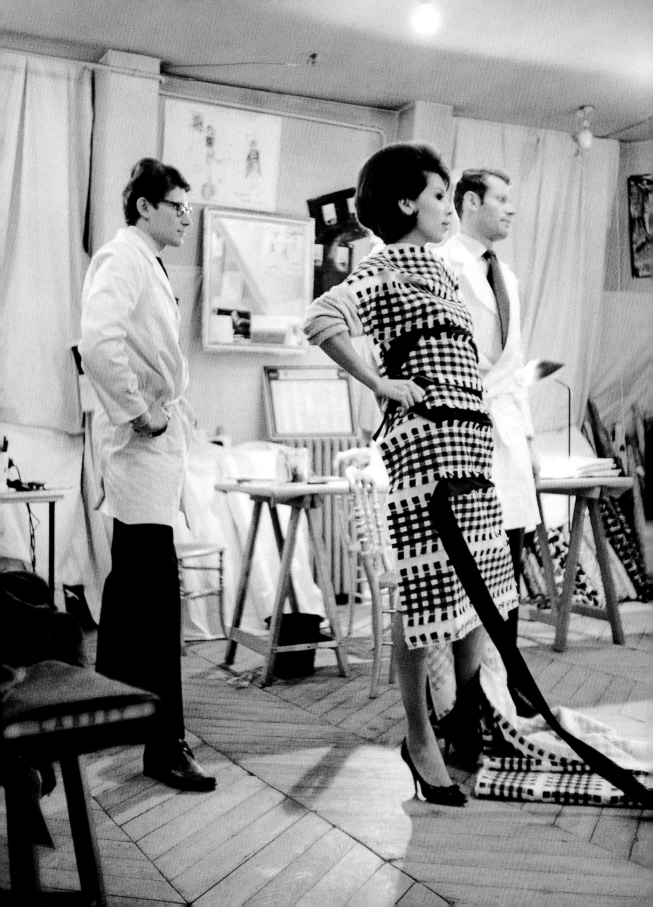

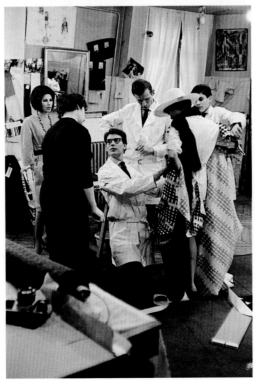

Were we scared?

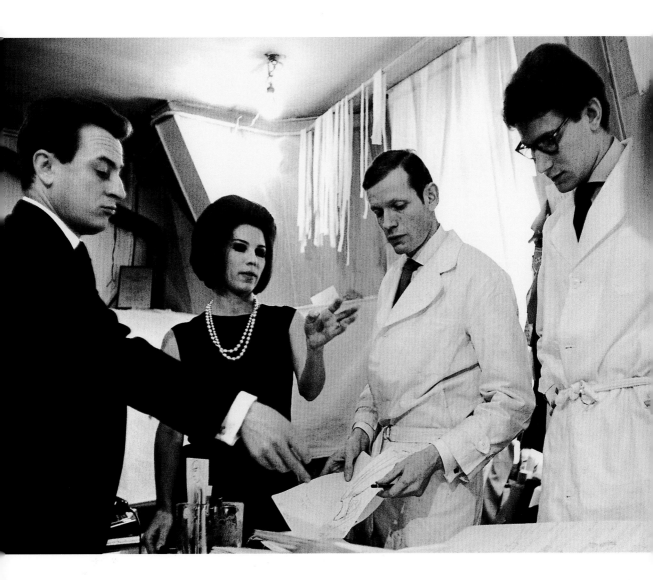

Everyone makes it their business.

OVERLEAF:

Ah! Lord, jewels everywhere!

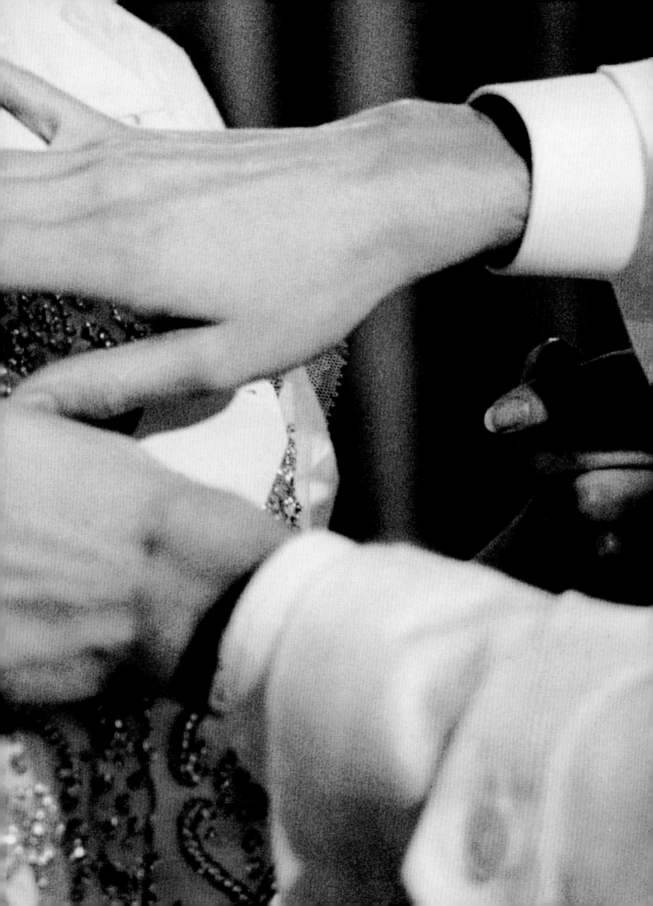

PREVIOUS SPREAD:

Yves's hands.

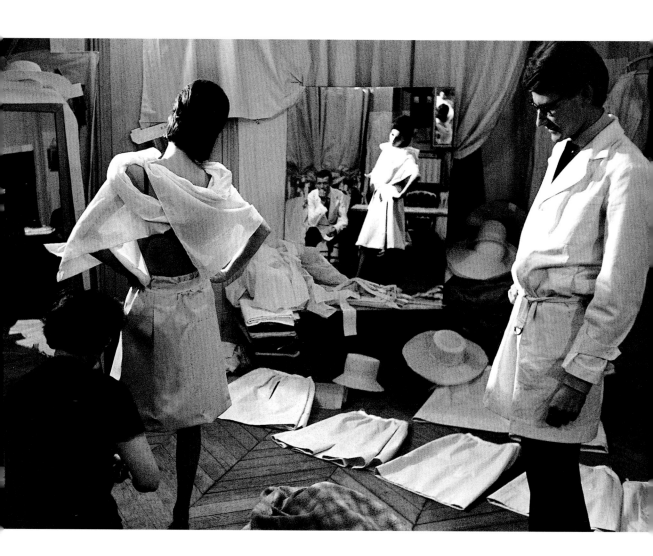

OVERLEAF:

A surgeon reassuring his patient.

PAGES 46–47:

Muslin takes off for the first time.

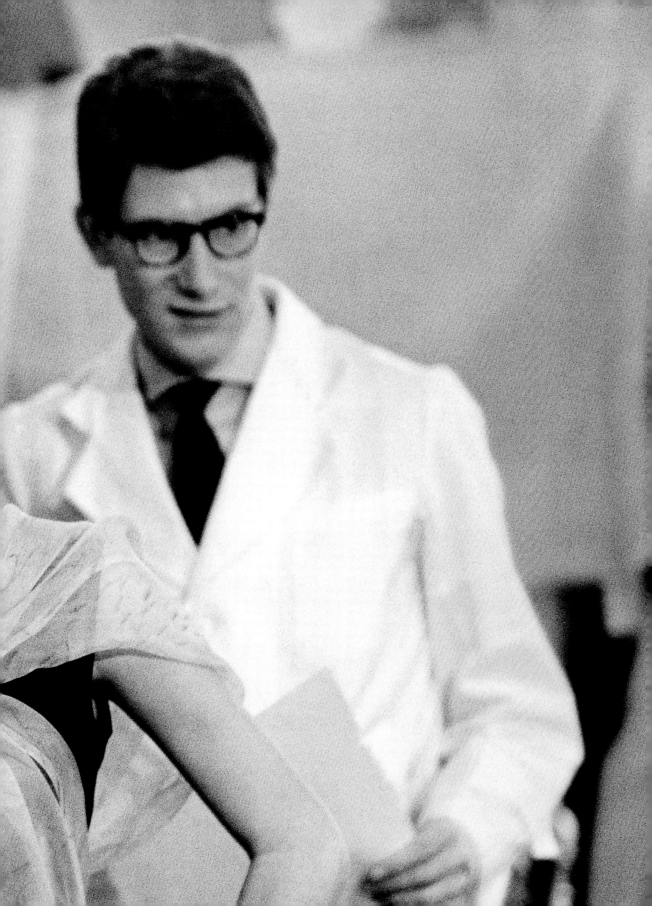

PREVIOUS SPREAD:

We would discover video.

A way to control fabric.

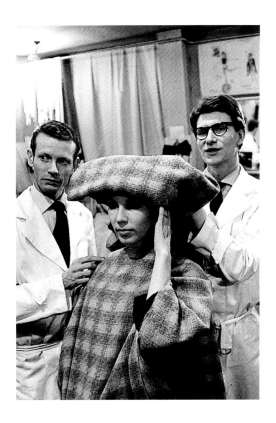

OVERLEAF:

An insect that's about to walk.

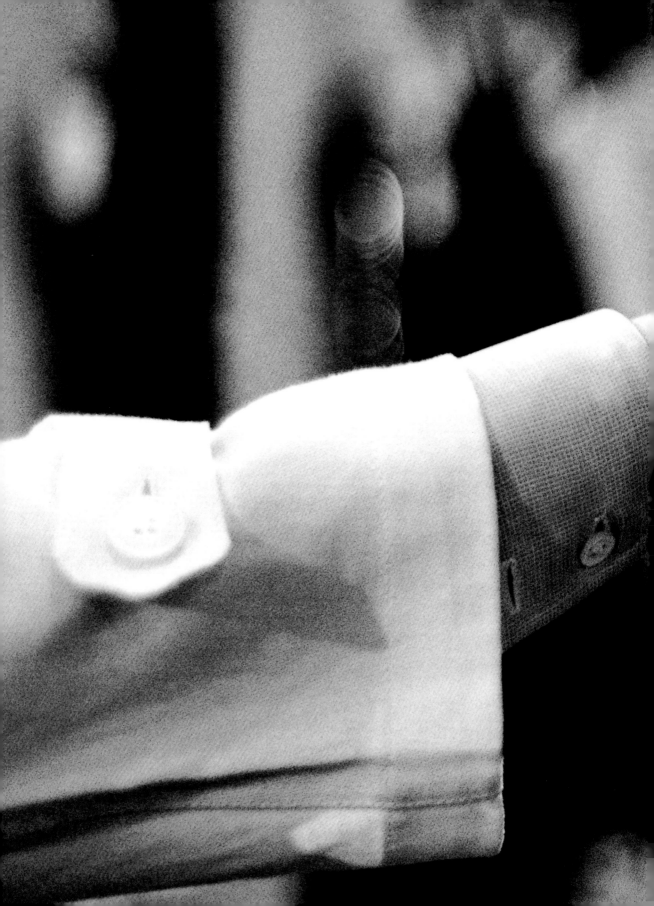

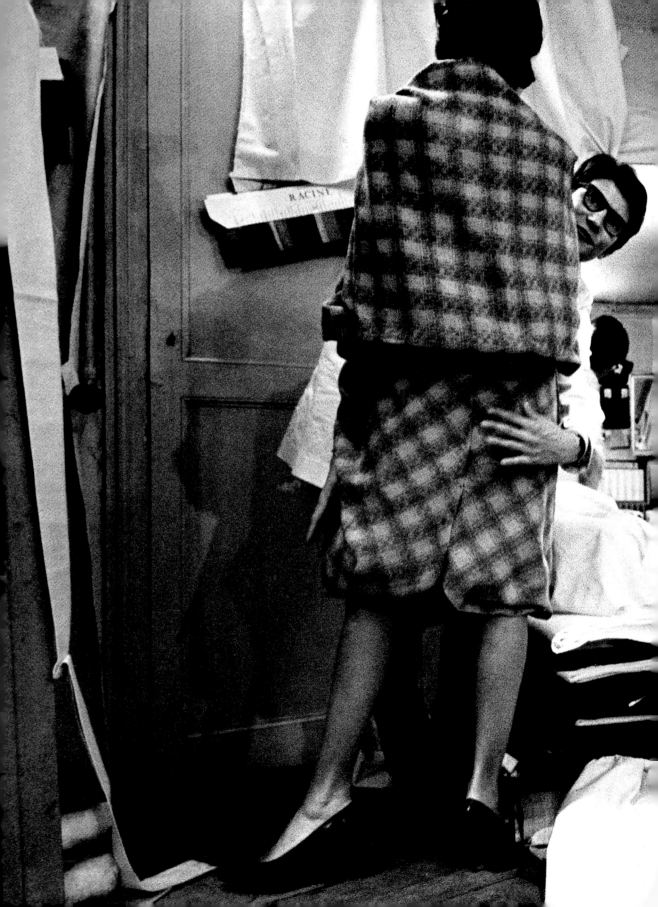

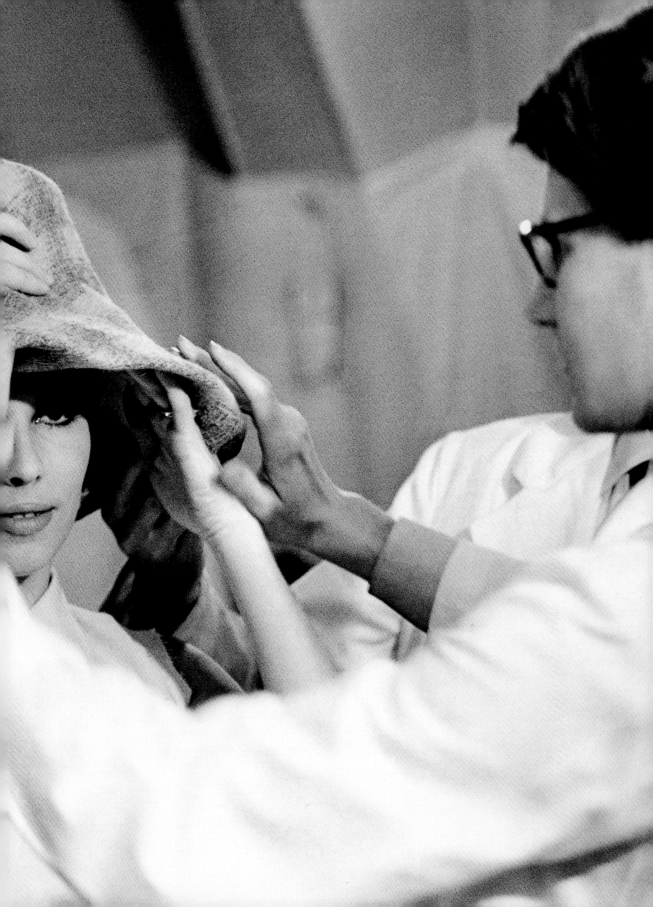

Only the beauty of the gestures.

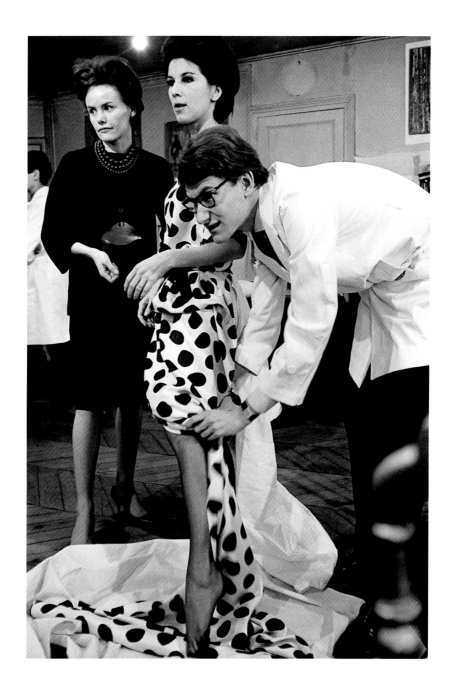

OVERLEAF:

Ready to fly away.

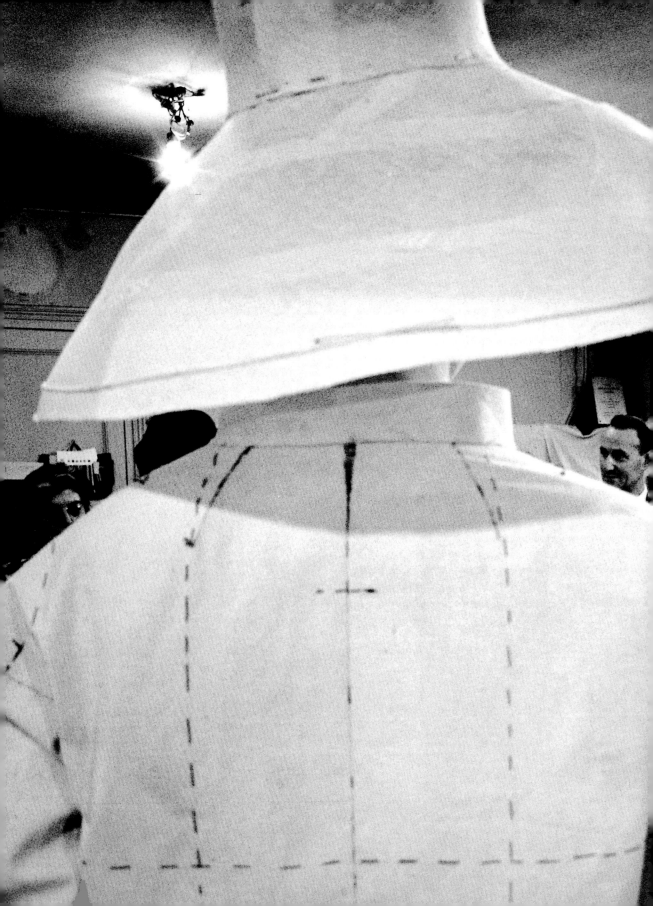

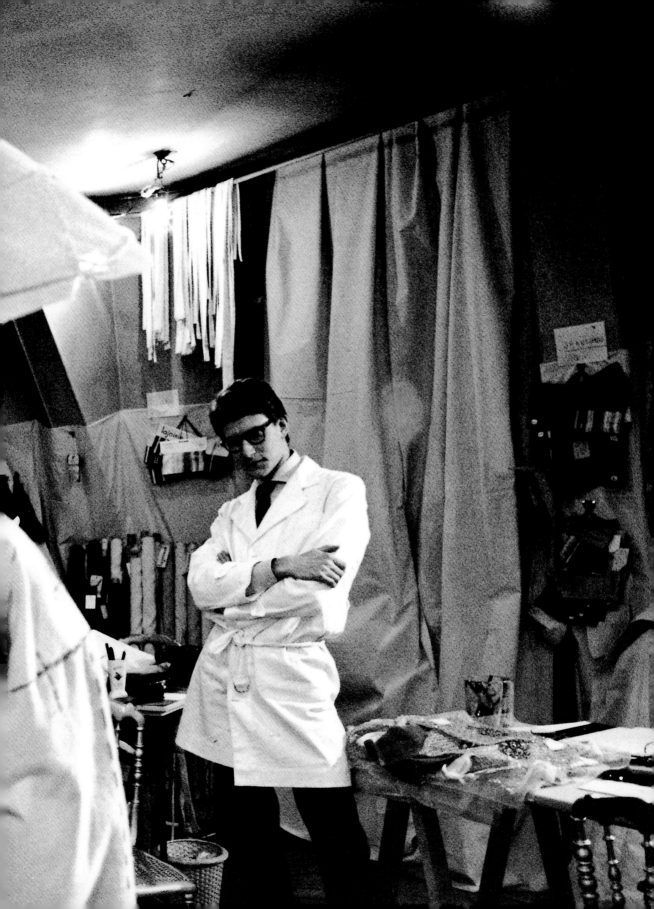

PREVIOUS SPREAD:

That day, he wasn't happy.

Cloth like an architect's floor plan.

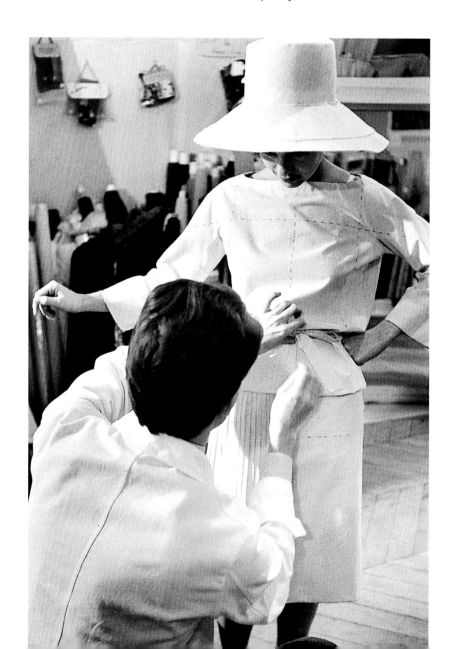

It's a good day.

PREVIOUS SPREAD:

The days go by.

Disturbing resemblance.

The hand that tames.

OVERLEAF:

Comparison is no reason.

PREVIOUS SPREAD:

Take a prisoner with a stare.

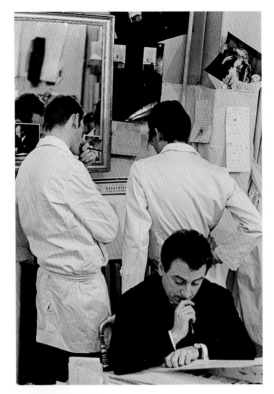

Yves Saint Laurent

We cross out every passing day.

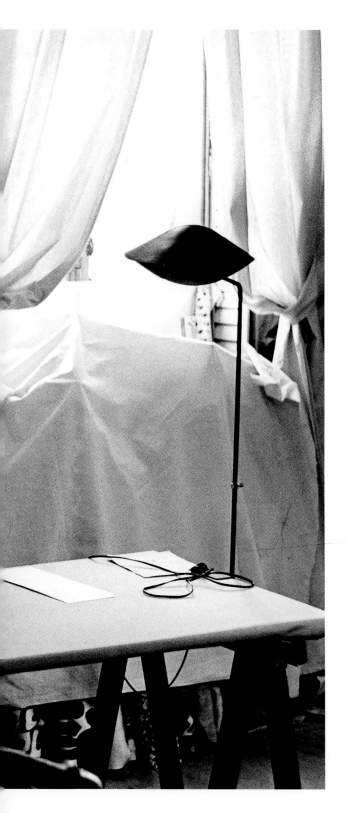

*And yet he's protected
by his master,
Christian Dior.*

Roland Petit's ballets.

Watched over by his bird, Senufo.

PREVIOUS SPREAD:

What are they thinking about?

Hazel, his first Chihuahua.

Victoire, Françoise Sagan, Yves, and others… An era.

*Say good-bye to
the gold chairs.*

A single eye to see everything.

It's done.

They're all there.

It's the night before the presentation.

The smile of a conqueror.

OVERLEAF:

Jesse Mack Robinson,
the man who believed.

Zizi Jeanmaire, who's just as anxious.

OVERLEAF:

In Zizi's arms, his victory brings tears to his eyes.

119

Yves Saint Laurent

This is how it all ends.

ACKNOWLEDGMENTS

To Monsieur Yves Saint Laurent and Monsieur Pierre Bergé

To Dominique Deroche from Yves Saint Laurent Haute Couture

To Richard Azoulay from Central Color